a Picture Postcard History of New York's Broome County Area

a Picture Postcard History of New York's Broome County Area

. . . Binghamton, Johnson City, Endicott, Owego, and
surrounding communities

compiled by
The Kiwanis Club of Binghamton, New York
in cooperation with the Vestal Press

The Vestal Press Ltd
- 1985 -

Library of Congress Cataloging-in-Publication Data
Main entry under title:

A Picture post-card history of New York's Broome
   County area—Binghamton, Johnson City, Endicott,
   Owego, and surrounding communities.

   1. Broome County (N.Y.)—History—Pictorial works. 2. Broome
County (N.Y.)—Description and travel—Views. 3. Postal cards—
New York (State)—Broome County. I. Kiwanis Club of Binghamton,
New York.
F127.B8P53   1985   974.7'75042   85-20880
ISBN 0-911572-48-1

For additional copies of this book or other publications, including a com-
plete catalog, write to The Vestal Press Ltd, PO Box 97, Vestal, New
York 13850 USA

FOREWORD

A fascinating way to gain a glimpse of how we Americans lived generations ago is easily afforded by the study of post-cards. Cards have been widely sold in America and around the World for close to a hundred years, and because they have been produced in such large numbers, there are plenty of them around to examine. The collecting of postcards has become a significant hobby, collectors tending to specialize in their favorite subject, such as trolley cars, amusement parks, churches, railroads, or whatever.

Those of us who live in the Broome County area are especially fortunate that a lot of cards were published, no doubt because there have been a lot of eminently artistic scenes at hand for the always-present photographers of every generation. From our parks and our churches to the numerous factories and commercial enterprises and schools, a lot has taken place here to build a firm foundation for today's 'high-tech' economy. Our magnificent natural scenery hasn't made the photographers job difficult, either!

This book is produced by members of the Kiwanis Club of Binghamton as a means a popularizing the picture history of our region, and at the same time providing a fund-raising effort that can be shared with other clubs and organizations throughout the community.

The Broome County Historical Society, as well as numerous individuals, went out of the way either to loan cards or to help gather information for this work. Thanks are due to Clayton and Katherine Ellis, William Lay, Ruth Axtell, Larry Leamer, Hilah Rounds, Gil Williams, Fred Goughary, Janet Ottman, Robert Murphy, Jim Fiori, Marie Scott, Chief William Grace, Rodney Ketcham, Craig O'Buckley, and last but not least, Marjorie Hinman—Librarian of the Historical Society—who was most generous not only of her time, but of her own research efforts that have appeared in several books she has written. Special thanks are due Mr. and Mrs. Greg Stella, of the firm Eastern Graphics, for their donation of the cover design which they did in recognition of her father, Richard G. Hill, and his long-time interest in the Kiwanis organization.

September, 1985

POSTCARD MEMORIES . . . . .

They don't make postcards, or "Postal Cards," the way they used to.

The late 20th century postcards are too slick, too influenced by newspaper and television photographs and films, too *sophisticated*, according to current tastes.

For a dreamy cruise through American scenes of the late 19th century and the early 20th, go aboard a craft that once dominated low-cost messages among friends, the American postcard. The craft was an honorable one, the tinted panoramas of the small towns and the big cities produced by men and women who were dedicated to the art of reproducing what America looked like during the period that preceded automatic cameras, cameras that even a child can use without making an error.

The early postcards of the United States were hand-tinted, if they were colored, or, after the development of early cameras, were in sepia or in black-and-white. That was important, but what was the most vital thing about early postcards is that they told what life was like.

In the 1980s, it is possible for a person with tugs on the historical lobes of his brain to look at these unforgettable scenes of a long-gone era depicting the main streets, the fashions, the dress and demeanor of men and women now dead, their recreational habits, their jobs, their home lives.

It is no wonder at all that the collecting of postcards has become a passion with many. They tell the story of an era we never will see again. In our case, in this book, we dwell pretty much on the local scene, which does not differ from the postcard scenes of any town in America.

The postcard is an institution as American as your Aunt Minnie was. It was Aunt Minnie, you remember, who you were discussing at your lakeside vacation when you suddenly said, "My gosh, I promised Aunt Minnie I'd send her a postcard! I'll do it first thing in the morning." Aunt Minnie was delighted when she got it, not only because you had remembered her, but she also enjoyed the rose-tinted hand-drawn sunset on the front of the card. Aunt Minnie always kept it in her Remembrance Book.

In the last 15 years of the 20th century, vacationers still are blurting, "Omygosh, I forgot to send Aunt Minnie a postcard!" and they go to the drug store to pick out scenes of their vacation spot and get them off in the mail immediately.

The postcard occupies a special place not only in American history, but in American tradition and the need for people to keep in touch with each other. It's a nice habit.

Tom Cawley

Tom Cawley died on October 21st of 1985, at the age of 72, thus making this commentary one of the very last—if not the last—of his journalistic contributions to Binghamton and the Broome County area to appear in print. His ability to use words of the English language to describe the news, the beauty, the people, and the character of the region earned the envy of all professional newspaper people who knew him or had worked with him in his long career with the news media of the community. His insightful comments will be long remembered by his thousands of loyal readers.

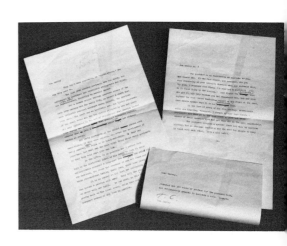

Done in the manner of the typical 'old-time' professional reporter is Tom's manuscript of the words above, done on a typewriter on scraps of newsprint.

The Harpursville Baptist Church was founded in 1811, and this building was built in 1846. The Harpursville Baptists built a new church in 1965 and this building has since been the Bethel Chapel. Note the sheds for horses in the rear.

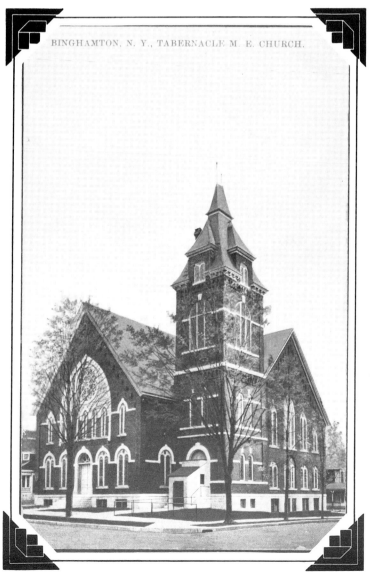

The Main Street Methodist Episcopal Church at Main and Arthur Street was completed and dedicated on September 19, 1884. The building and furnishings exclusive of the site which cost $11,500, ran $42,442.63. The architect was T. I. Lacey; the builder W. D. Stevens. With a cut stone foundation, brick walls and Onondaga limestone trimmings, it is semi-gothic in style. The west tower was originally 100 feet high, and the east tower 70 feet high. The original steeple was removed in 1935, when it required extensive repairs. It became the Tabernacle M.E. Church on September 29, 1928.

BINGHAMTON, N. Y., COR. MAIN AND FRONT STS.

In 1840 an organization known as the "M.E. Protestant Church of Binghamton" established itself at the corner of Court and Carroll Streets, but was disbanded about ten years later. A second society was formed in 1851 and led by Rev. Thomas Pearne, pastor of the First Methodist Episcopal Church, who in 1865 formed the Centenary Church. Dr. Bristol succeeded Mr. Pearne in 1866 and a new church building was erected in 1866-68 on its present site, at a cost of $65,000. Numerous subsequent improvements have greatly enhanced the value of the church's plant. A number of other churches in the area owe their beginnings to its surplus spiritual strength, the Tabernacle Church being one example.

The First Congregational Church (United Church of Christ) is on the site of Peterson's Tavern, the first meeting place of the newly-incorporated Village of Binghamton on May 3, 1834. Like many other buildings in the city, it was designed by Isaac Perry; it was completed in 1869, at a cost of $57,000. J. Stuart Wells was the builder. The lofty spire of the structure was damaged by a windstorm during the 1920s, and had to be removed.

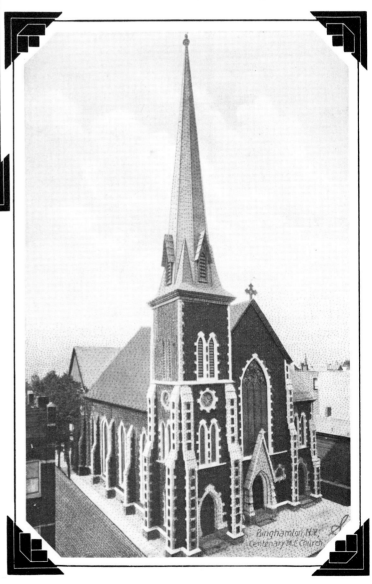

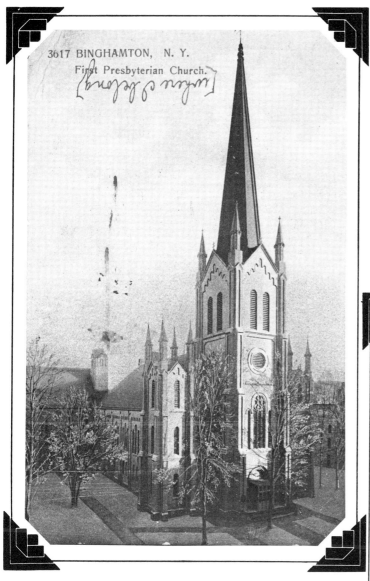

3617 BINGHAMTON, N. Y.
First Presbyterian Church.

Miles Leonard was the builder of Binghamton's First Baptist Church in 1872, to designs by architect T. I. Lacey. It was rebuilt after a fire in 1893, and was demolished in 1970 to build the 100 Chenango Street apartment complex.

FIRST BAPTIST CHURCH, BINGHAMTON, N. Y.

The first edifice the Presbyterians had was built on the present site and was dedicated for worship on January 1, 1820. It was enlarged in 1832, 1843, and 1848. Later, a short distance away, a new Romanesque style building was erected to accomodate 1200 persons. On the Sunday night immediately preceeding the Sabbath set for the opening, it burned to the ground. The church, under the leadership of Pastor Dr. Boardman, was re-built and dedicated on April 26th, 1863. It is regarded by many as one of the most beautiful and stately churches in the country. A decade later, a north wing was built; a children's chapel, classrooms, and a kitchen have been added. The First Presbyterian Church is the mother of several other churches. In 1836, a group of its members spun off to form the nucleus of the First Congregational Church.

St. Patrick's Church and St. Joseph's Convent, Binghampton, N.Y.

Father James Hourigan, who had emigrated from the 'auld sod', became the pastor of the parish in the late 1840's, and he served when the structure seen in this picture was dedicated in 1873. Isaac Perry was the architect, and his design featured a lofty steeple which in later years had to be removed because some of the wooden structure had rotted. Note the spelling of 'Binghampton'. Many of the postcards in this book from the early 20th century were made in Germany, and this error seems to be fairly common on cards of that period.

The first services held in Trinity Memorial Church were on June 13, 1886. The house at the right was the home of Dr. Leroy D. Farnham from 1886 to 1915, and the Rev. W. E. Tanner from 1918 to 1930; the educational wing of the church now occupies this spot. Note the tracks of the Leroy Street trolley line making the corner from Oak Street onto Main.

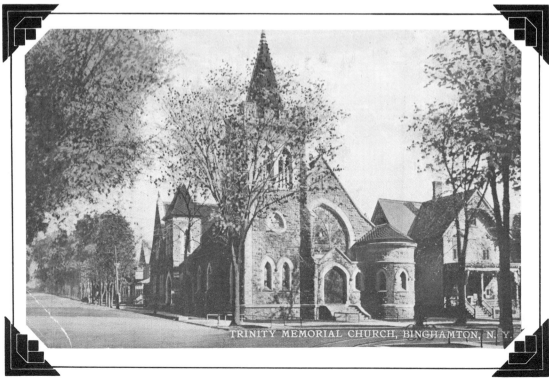

TRINITY MEMORIAL CHURCH, BINGHAMTON, N. Y.

Sky Lake of Wyoming Conference, Windsor, N. Y.

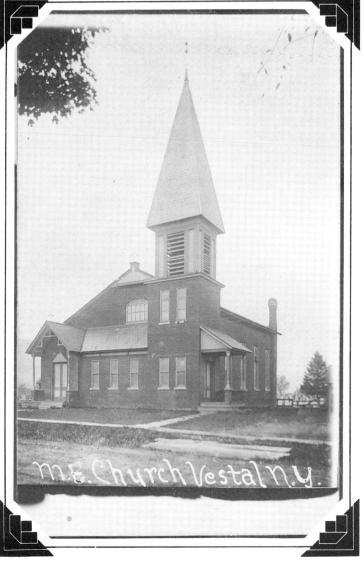

M.E. Church Vestal N.Y.

Sky Lake and its lodge were formerly owned by Willis Sharpe Kilmer, and were purchased by the Methodist Conference in 1947. They added a dining room in 1955, and a new lodge was added in 1965.

This was the first Methodist Church in Broome County, and was built prior to 1845. The original acre site was purchased for $100 from Daniel and Abigil Foster in 1834, and part of the land is now the adjacent cemetery. The structure was damaged in 1902 in that terrific explosion of the carload of dynamite on the Lackawanna Railroad, and $800 had to be spent to put the place back in shape. While most of the steeples on churches in the county were removed by an itinerant construction firm that specialized in this work, the Good Lord took care of this unusual-shaped one with a lighting bolt on 30 August, 1921, which not only destroyed it but the front of the building as well. In 1922 the sanctuary was enlarged and classrooms were added. In 1948 the name was changed for the third time, to the Vestal Methodist Church, and the term 'Methodist Episcopal' no longer applies.

M. E. CHURCH, COR. COLLINS & LIBERTY ST., WHITNEY POINT, N. Y.

The original Church building of the Methodist Episcopal congregation in Whitney Point was constructed in 1843; it was rebuilt in 1868, and again in 1899 after the great fire even though it was not damaged in that conflagration. The house in the rear of the picture is the parsonage, which was built in 1898 for Luke English. It was owned by F. C. Branday, publisher of the Whitney Point Reporter, who sold it to the Methodist Church.

The Practical Bible Training School is built on the former site of Wagner Park or the White City Amusement Park, on Riverside Drive in Johnson City. The school has operated here since 1910. This building is the former casino, with at least one addition; it has been replaced by a modern structure. Note the address given as 'Bible School Park'; a post office has operated here for many years.

Practical Bible Training School, Bible School Park, N. Y.

The Congregational Church on Rt. 26 in Maine was organized in 1819, and this building was built in 1840. When the Maine Methodist-Episcopal Church burned in 1928 the congregation joined with the Congregationalists to form the Federated Church of Maine.

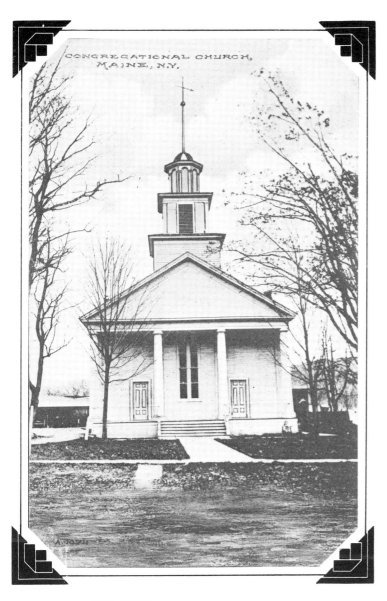

Under the supervision of Dr. Oliver Bundy of Deposit, who had been a Surgeon in the 144th Regiment in the Civil War, a monument committee was formed, and its cost was met by appropriations of $1,000 by each of the towns of Tompkins (now Town of Deposit) and Sanford—together with private contributions of $750. The monument was dedicated on Thursday, September 27, 1888, and as we see here, it is adjacent to what the card refers as the 'Episcopale' Church. The cornerstone of the church was laid on June 23, 1892.

The Methodist Episcopal Church of Lestershire (1891-1925)—now the Sarah Jane Johnson Memorial—is at the left in this photo. The First Baptist Church (1891-1924), is at the right. They preceeded the present structures at Main and Baldwin Streets in Johnson City; land for both was donated by G. Harry Lester.

Methodist and Baptist Churches, LESTERSHIRE, N. Y.

FIRST PRESBYTERIAN CHURCH, JOHNSON CITY, N. Y.

On May 22, 1892, the Floral Avenue Presbyterian Church of Binghamton was organized with 43 members, meeting in a simple chapel building. Subsequently a parlor was added to the chapel, as seen at the left of the stone structure in this postcard shot. In 1915 a decision was made concerning a new church, with a construction cost estimate of $14,170. The Johnson family, of E-J fame, offered a donation of $10,000 towards a $30,000 structure, providing it be built in Johnson City. Apparently this financial help was contingent upon a name change, so it became the First Presbyterian Church of Johnson City. By the time the church was finally paid for, in 1943, total costs (including a manse and interest) came to over $123,000. On October 21, 1916, at the ceremony for the cornerstone laying which took place during construction, the floor, along with many people, crashed into the basement. While there were many injuries, no one was critically hurt.

High School, WINDSOR, N. Y.

The Windsor Academy and High School was built in 1883 on Academy Street. The addition of the "recitation room" at the right was made in 1893. Teacher training classes and summer "Teacher's Institutes" were held here. The building was used as a school until 1933, after which it was utilized as American Legion Post #591, and finally as a sanctuary for Our Lady of Lourdes Church. Demolished in 1970 to build a fire station.

This pin-connected truss was built in 1879 to replace a covered bridge over the Susquehanna River, by the Corrugated Iron Company of E. Berlin, Connecticut, at a cost of about $20,000. The sign reads: "$5 Fine for Driving Faster Than A Walk Across the Bridge". Its intent was to minimize the rhythm of the horses hooves which could cause the structure to sway. The bridge was used until 1902.

4—Looking Through the Bridge, Windsor, N Y.

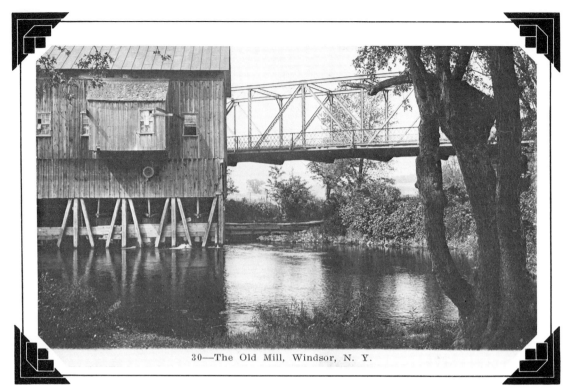

30—The Old Mill, Windsor, N. Y.

The grist mill at the end of Bridge Street. The water in the picture is the raceway; the Susquehanna River is at the right of the island.

The Windsor Village Green was donated to the Presbyterian Church by David Hotchkiss around 1800 when the first church was built in the center of the Green.

In 1840, due to a controversy over the slavery question, there was a split in the church, and each faction built a new church on the Green in 1842. Ten years later they reconciled their differences and united in the church on the left. The other was briefly used by the Baptists from 1858, and then by the Free Methodists since 1872. The band pagoda was built in 1880. The present pagoda utilizes the same intricate roof as the old.

The Park, WINDSOR, N. Y.

Empire State Whip Co. Factory, Windsor, N. Y.

A great American tradition is that of 'Old Home Week' even though it may not be quite clear to the local citizens as to just what the term actually means! In any event, in this scene in Windsor from the 'teens there's no shortage of fine bunting and flag-waving, all designed to instill a measure of pride in those who were born and raised in the community which they could always call "home", regardless of where they might reside at the time of the event. This scene is from the celebration which took place in 1914.

Buggy whip-making was the industry of the Industrial Revolution in Windsor, with the Empire State Whip Company being one of several. Windsor was second only to New York City in production of these essentials in the day of horse power. Whips were made in Windsor from 1854 until 1951, the later whips being produced as souvenirs for circuses.

Upper Main Street,
WINDSOR, N. Y.

Main Street, route 79, looking south. Brownell's Furniture (left building) became Chase's Furniture and Undertaking, the beginning of a long Chase family business. This building became the Windsor Bank in 1915, and a branch of the Marine Midland Bank in 1966. Next is the Windsor Town and Village Hall, built in 1904 for $8,000. The third structure was built by the Masons as an apartment house, and they had their hall on the third floor.

The building in this scene was razed in 1913 for a new structure which was dedicated in 1914, and which now serves as an elementary school. The one seen here replaced the "Academy" building, which had been built around 1885 under the direction of Professor Nevius.

Deposit High School.
DEPOSIT, N. Y.

PUBL. BY
LESLIE E. CARL

Deposit 7-4-06.

Copyright, 1906, by Leslie E. Carl, Jeweler, Deposit, N. Y.

VILLAGE HALL AND FIRE STATION,
FRONT STREET, DEPOSIT, N. Y.

I am stopping at this place for a while. W

The Deposit Village Hall on Front Street was built around 1899. It housed the fire station until it was renovated in the early 1970's for Town and Village offices and the Police Station.

The first Erie station at Deposit, a wooden frame building, stood on land bought from Uriah Gregory in 1849. This burned and was replaced with this brick depot in 1861, at a cost of $10,305. Many local citizens were outraged when Conrail in March 1981, without any advance notice, levelled this station with bulldozers. This was a sad day for historic preservation, particularly since the Erie Railroad was started in Deposit in November of 1835.

Erie Depot and Square, Deposit, N. Y.

13

Fortner's Store, in McClure, New York, on the corner of what we know today as Route 41 and old Route 17, was built by Will and Bess Fortner around 1885. It passed to a daughter, Gwendolyn Fortner Nolan, and her husband 'Mickey', and they sold it around 1976. Since then it has been greatly altered, and 100 years after its construction, the business has fallen into bankruptcy. It is said that the four Fortner daughters—Reva, Gwendolyn, Edna, and Donna—always clung to their mother's long skirt when she went from the living quarters into the store.

Hanson's Resort on Oquaga Lake was first known as "Retlaw", which is the name Walter spelled backwards. John Q. Walter of Deposit was the owner. At the time of preparation of this book, Hanson's had been turned into an apartment house. In the 1970's Ed Link, Binghamton's famed inventor, built a steamboat patterned after the one seen here.

Scott's Oquaga Lake House has been entertaining guests since 1880, and currently is operated by the fourth generation of the family. One of its attractions is the absence of liquor for sale on the premises. Many tourists from Canada, arriving by the busload, are a mainstay of its clientele.

Oquaga Lake House, Oquaga Lake, N.Y.

SULPHO-PHOSPHATE SPRING AT
Dr. S. Andral Kilmer's Sanitarium-in-the-Mountains, Sanitaria Springs, N. Y.

Dr. Kilmer's Sanitarium-in-the-Mountains was also known as Kilmer's Watercure Sanitorium, and he also called it a "Cancertorium". It was built in 1892 in Osborne Hollow (later Sanitaria Springs). It ceased to operate around 1929 when water therapy was no longer popular.

Dr. S. Andral Kilmer's Sanitarium-in-the-Mountains, Sanitaria Springs, N. Y.

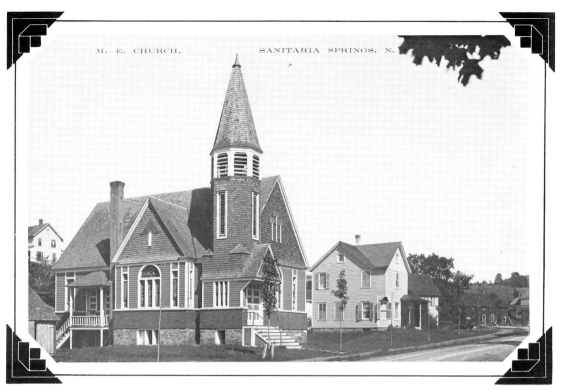

The Sanitaria Springs Methodist Church was built in 1893 on the site of the first church, which had been built in 1847. It continues to serve the community. Sanitaria Springs was first called Osborne's Hollow, but Dr. S. Andral Kilmer changed it when he built his sanitarium in 1893.

The four corners in Harpursville, looking west. The "New York Cash Store" on the right was operated for many years as a general store by William E. Knox. It has continued to the present to serve the community.

17

17—D. & H. Sta. and Borden's, Harpursville, N. Y.

The Harpursville Delaware and Hudson Railroad Station and the creamery were located on a hill between Harpursville and Afton. A horsedrawn omnibus took people to and from the village. In the 1870's this was known as a shipping point for butter.

Eldorado House, HARPURSVILLE, N. Y.

The Eldorado House in Harpursville was built in 1825, and was destroyed by fire in 1933. In the 1876 Broome County Atlas, the drawing of the Eldorado carries the caption "S. J. Groat, Proprietor. Livery Attached, charges reasonable, carriage for guests at all trains." The Harpursville Fire Station now occupies the site.

THE MILK STATION, WHITNEY POINT, N. Y.

The F. W. Janssen creamery, as shown here was taken over by The Borden Company, and during the 1930's and 1940's was part of the Dairyman's League organization. It was destroyed by a fire in March of 1961. Note what is probably the early morning milk train, poised for a quick dash to the metropolitan market with the products of the farmers of the area around Whitney Point. For many years the transportation of milk to the New York City area provided a major source of income for railroads of the region, of which this Lackawanna consist on the Cortland and Oswego branch stemming northward from Binghamton is a typical example.

DENNING'S STORE AND POST OFFICE, WHITNEY POINT, N. Y.

These structures still stand, and look much the same today as they did when William Denning published this postcard—probably around 1920, to judge by the automobile in the scene. The Post Office moved to its new location in 1961, and a beauty shop is now located where it had been. Whitney Point Wholesale Meats is now located in Denning's Store. These buildings—the Page Block and the Wilcox Block—were constructed in 1898 following the great fire of 1897. The third floor of the Wilcox Block serves as a Masonic Lodge, the only use to which it has been put.

19

After the fire in 1901 that destroyed the old Whitney Point school, the bandstand located on the front lawn of the school was moved to the fair ground to become the judging stand. It was removed from the fairground in 1973. The grandstand at the left was built in 1899, and was demolished in 1973 to make way for a new one of steel construction. The fair was inaugurated in 1874, and has been held every year since except for during World War 2. This photo dates from the very early 1900's when the community was still called "Whitney's Point."

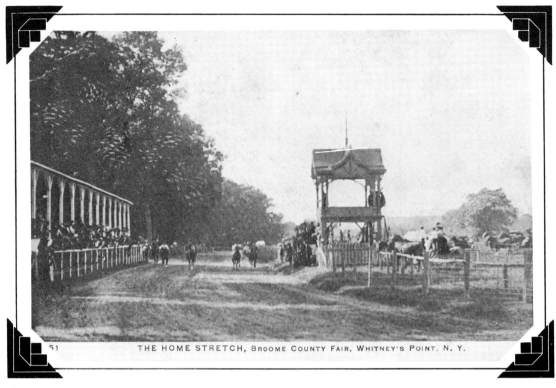

51   THE HOME STRETCH, BROOME COUNTY FAIR, WHITNEY'S POINT, N. Y.

This Whitney Point High School was approved by the voters on April 11, 1901, to replace a wooden building lost in a 1900 fire. It was constructed of brick and stone, had a slate roof, and steam heat and electricity were featured. The approved cost was not to exceed $15,000, and the low bid was $12,200. The structure withstood the 1935 flood, but was taken out of school use on December 1, 1936. It housed several small businesses after this, and the Farmers Home Administration occupied it before it was torn down in 1961. The small building at the rear was the Annex, known as the "chicken coop" by the students.

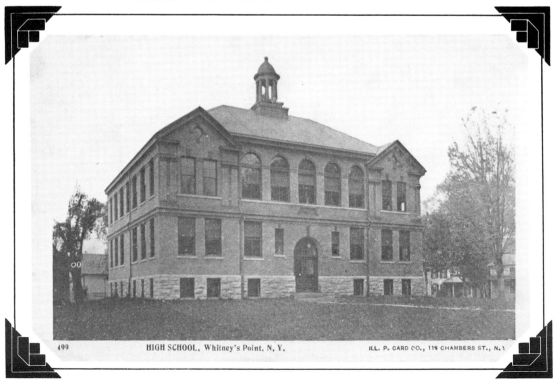

499   HIGH SCHOOL, Whitney's Point, N. Y.   ILL. P. CARD CO., 118 CHAMBERS ST., N. Y

Ninevah is partly in Broome County and partly in Chenango County. Its chief industry from 1845 until 1920 was the Hobbs Carriage Works and later the Ninevah Coach and Car Company, for they made the transition from carriages and wagons to automobiles. This scene is around 1910.

THE SUSQUEHANNA, NEW BRIDGE, AND SECTION OF NINEVEH, N. Y. (S. W.)

AIRVIEW OF (So. Side) CHENANGO FORKS, N. Y.

This postcard dates from the Bi-Centennial year of 1976, showing the Chenango Forks community from the South. The bridges are over the Tioghnioga River before it flows into the Chenango River. On this side of the river is the town of Chenango; that part of the community on the far side of the river is in the town of Barker. The railway overpass seen here is from the 1930's; it was replaced in 1984.

Club House on Chenango Valley State Park Golf Course, Binghamton, N. Y.

The golf course at Chenango Valley State Park was built under a Federal Work program, and it opened in 1936, with 9 holes, and Lynn Higgs the Pro the first year. Ralph Hathaway was the Professional Golfer on hand for many subsequent years, and the course was enlarged to 18 holes in 1968, during his tenure.

Itaska, first called Fuller Settlement, is located off route 79 across the Tioghnioga River, south of Whitney Point. Today it looks much the same as this scene, except of course for the Lackawanna passenger train with its 'camelback' locomotive. The large barn at center left is on the Klein farm and is still in use today. The long white building at the right was the depot and a feed store which was partially destroyed by fire some years ago. It is still in use today, but as a residence. The Lackawanna Railroad burned hard coal (anthracite), which required a very large grate area in the locomotive fireboxes. This left little room for the engineer to do his job, so the 'camelback' engine was developed which placed the controls of the machine in a cab located midway down the length of the boiler. The fireman of course still shoveled coal from his station in a cab at the rear of the locomotive.

Lisle Academy, Main St. Lisle, N. Y.

The Lisle Academy building was torn down in 1953. The bell from the top of the building is now located on the Lisle Village Green on Main Street. This school was one of the more well-known ones of its day; one celebrity who attended it for a time was H. H. Franklin who lived in Center Lisle and who went on to build the Franklin automobile in Syracuse.

In 1985 Vestal residents could be proud of the fact that their school system was judged by experts to be one of the best in the entire United States, according to an article that appeared in The Evening Press! In 1881-2 the system was privileged to be housed in this modest building which was built by Silas Twilliger. It had two rooms and a recitation room, and as was typical of the day in small communities, several grades were taught by a teacher in one room. The structure was razed in 1952 after it had served as a community hall, and some of the lumber was used to construct a Boy Scout Lodge on Foster Road.

Located across the street from G. W. Crane's store was Will Pierce's store, which was the same sort of place except that meat was not sold by him. Mrs. Pierce did not work in the store, which was open from 7 AM to dark. The Pierce living quarters were in the building on the right side, and the second floor of the store building was used for storage. Note the sheds in the rear. Pierce, being a Republican, had the Post Office in his place of business when that party was in power. It is said that Pierce and Crane were strong rivals with loyal customers; families which dealt with Pierce, who did not sell meat, would buy their meat in Union rather than to deal with his competitor right across the street.

George W. Crane was a Democrat, and when that party was in power, the Vestal Post Office was in his general store. The store was built around 1890, sometime after the meat market seen elsewhere in this book, and he sold dry goods, hardware, and all types of food including meats. His family (which may be the group on the porch) had living quarters on the second floor of this building, located at Main and Front Streets—right across from a major competitor, W. S. Pierce. The store was generally open from 7 AM to dark, with Mr. Crane alone. Mrs. Crane did not work in the store.

24

On April 15 of 1927 a real mess was created on the main intersection in Vestal by a fire which destroyed the Frey Drug Store and a large general store. The ruins are plainly visible in this aerial photo that was made into a postcard. Soon after this disaster a municipal water department was created, to assist in controlling any future events of this nature that might befall the town.

Around the turn of the Century Vestal had a distinctive rural flavor, as seen in this view looking north from the beginning of Front Street. The Pierce building is at the left, with the Rounds Coal Company in the distance. The Crane building is the first one at the right of the picture.

Main Street, Vestal, N. Y.

J. S. Crane built this meat market in 1860, at the corner of Front and Main Streets in Vestal. The second floor of the building was used for storage, and his living quarters were the home seen at the right.

Local residents of Vestal pass the time of day in front of the village blacksmith shop which at one time was owned and operated by George Hill.

Vestal's Lackawanna Railroad Station was built in 1881, on ground purchased from Jacob L. Rounds, and his son Fayette Rounds was the first station agent. The first train to run through Vestal was on October 3, 1882. Note the east-bound train in the distance, and the water-plug served by the tower on the north side of the twin tracks. The small structures near the engine are sheds for housing the tools used by maintenance workers; one for the crew working east of Vestal, and the other for those toiling to the west. There was intense competition between the railway labor gangs for recognition and rewards for quality of their work, and it has been said that the rivalry was such that the two gangs were not even on speaking terms! To the delight of all rail fans and historically-minded citizens, the Vestal Town Board purchased the station from the Erie-Lackawanna Railroad after the merger of those two companies resulted in the tracks from Binghamton ending at Vestal. It was moved about a mile to the east, where it now serves as The Vestal Museum.

Fayette L. Rounds built this 15-room home in 1895, and it featured seven bedrooms on two floors and three more in the attic. Located on the corner of Pumphouse and Main (Bridge) Streets, it is still occupied by a descendant, Miss Hilah Rounds who provided interesting anecdotal material for this book. This photo, which was taken about 1920, faces east. Note the windmill in the back, which pumped water into the tank for use in the home.

Construction on the Endicott - Johnson Worker's Arch in Johnson City was started on August 14, 1919. According to a newspaper article on the 16th, "The foundation work was done by a squad of 15 men under the direction of Joseph McWenie. Lettering was done by George Shapley." The crumbling arch was rehabilitated in the early 1980's through the efforts of the Johnson City Jaycees.

E. J. WORKERS' ARCH AND MAIN STREET, JOHNSON CITY, N. Y.

MAIN STREET, LOOKING WEST, LESTERSHIRE, N. Y.

Horace Lester came from Haddam, CT, in 1850 to Binghamton and started a retail shoe business. His brother George joined him in 1854 to start the boot and shoe manufacturing firm of Lester Brothers & Co. on Court Street near Washington; they operated in downtown Binghamton for 25 to 30 years. They had the Lester Building on Washington, Henry, and State Streets, which later became part of the Hotel Bennett. Horace Lester died in 1882, and his son George took his place in the firm. He conceived the idea of a new factory outside the city, and in 1888 he purchased from several individuals a number of acres of farmland west of the city; this was to become Lestershire. In 1889 the Lestershire Boot and Shoe Company was incorporated and erected a large factory on the north side of the DL and W Railroad tracks. Other businesses soon followed and within a year a flourishing hamlet came into existence. On September 15, 1892, the Village of Lestershire, which included an area of 638.4 acres of land, was incorporated. This post card was postmarked in 1906, just 14 years after the event.

Residence and Grounds of Harry E. Brigham, Lestershire, N. Y.

Harry Brigham was the son of Elijah Waldo Brigham, who ran a successful brickyard business in Lestershire. The residence seen here was built around 1885, and was purchased in 1917 by the Endicott-Johnson Corporation through the personal interests of Harry L. Johnson, for use as a library for the benefit of E-J workers as well as the general public. It has always been known as 'Your Home Library.' Note in the library picture the added porches and the annex in the rear, as well as the large awnings which were helpful for personal comfort in pre-air-conditioning days. The annex was added in 1920, and housed a kitchen, a dining room, and a children's room, as the corporation wished the building to serve as a community center. In the late 1930's the Village took over the operation from the Endicott-Johnson Corporation.

YOUR HOME LIBRARY, JOHNSON CITY, N. Y.

29

FIRST NATIONAL BANK, & Y. M. C, A. BLDG, LESTERSHIRE, N. Y.   PUBL. BY LESTER ART ₁O ₂'

The First National Bank of Lestershire was built in 1904. In 1916 when the name of the community was changed to Johnson City, George F. Johnson suggested that the bank change its name to Worker's Trust, a title which remains to this day. The bank moved to a new location in 1932; Loft's Card and Gift Shop and Tom and Jerry's Wines and Liquors currently occupy the site, which is no longer a corner location. The Record Block

was built in 1902, the home of The Lestershire Record, William H. Hill's newspaper. The Ash Block stems from the same era. Mr. Hill was known locally as 'Mr. Republican' for many years, and he had the distinct honor of placing in nomination the name of Herbert Hoover for the U. S. Presidency at the National Republican Convention.

In 1899 George F. Johnson, who had been a superintendent in Henry B. Endicott's shoe factory, purchased a half-interest for $150,000. Endicott loaned Johnson, who had little or no money, the entire amount on a personal note! The firm name was changed to the Endicott-Johnson Shoe Company, and it ultimately became a major factor in the shoe industry, with employment in the neighborhood of 20,000 in the Triple Cities. Endicott-Johnson performed all operations in the manufacture of its shoes— the cutting operation being one. This view was taken close to the turn of the century.

CUTTING ROOM HEAVY WORK SHOE FACTORY, ENDICOTT, JOHNSON & CO., LESTERSHIRE, N. Y.
The secret of Better Shoes for Less Money is in an economical system of manufacturing. The power cutting machines shown in the illustration make a great saving over the old fashioned hand cutting method.

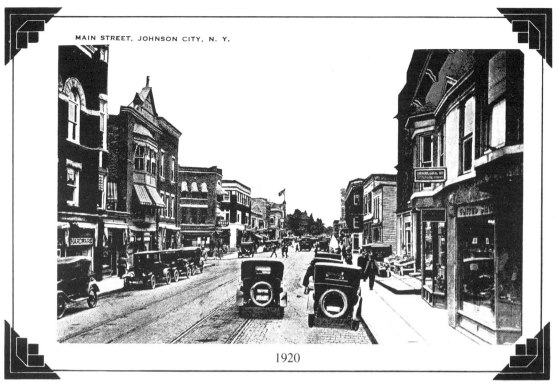

MAIN STREET, JOHNSON CITY, N. Y.

1920

Brick street paving was the order of the day, to replace mud and dirt, as automobiles became popular and more and more within the reach of the common man. Already one could predict from this ca. 1920 scene, free of curbside meters, that parking would eventually become a major headache not only for Johnson City, but for almost every other community across the land. Notice that once again, as in so many post card views, an artist has carefully air-brushed away the overhead wires that power the trolley cars—a trick commonly employed by graphic artists to make the scene appear more attractive than it actually was.

1923

BIRD'S EYE VIEW SHOWING ANSCO CAMERA WORKS, JOHNSON CITY, N. Y.

The Ansco Camera Works was brought to Lestershire in 1910. The name stems form the Anthony and Scoville firm which was formed in the mid-1800's; it eventually came under the control of the I. G. Farben interests in Germany, and was seized by the United States Government at the beginning of World War II. The sharp-eyed reader will note that the building is the same structure as seen on page 37, the Marshall Furniture factory.

Goodwill Theatre and Central Fire Station, Johnson City, N. Y.

The Goodwill Theatre was built by the Endicott-Johnson Corporation and opened around 1921, to provide low-cost entertainment for the shoe workers. Billy Mack was the manager for many years, and it is said that he was a difficult man to work for—insisting, for example, that Bill Riley, the organist, work a seven day week for long periods of time! It was considered quite a fine theatre in its day, and it boasted a Binghamton-built Beman two-manual pipe organ which featured an echo organ built in the dome of the main auditorium, as well as the usual drums and traps and other noise-makers typical of the theatre instruments of the era. Movies, stage shows, and vaudeville were the order of the day, and many individuals and groups of local telent performed there as well. The E-J Minstrels and the E-J Band with its famous Sunday night concerts were featured attractions. The name was changed to the En-Joie Theatre some years after its opening.

COASTER AT WHITE CITY, BINGHAMTON, N.Y.

White City was not, as stated on the postcard, in Binghamton. It was on Riverside Drive in Lestershire, on the banks of the Susquehanna River, and was a popular amusement park around the turn of the century and the early 1900's. During the summer months large throngs assembled to ride the roller coaster and to enjoy the other amusements. Prior to becoming White City

105:- SWIMMING POOL, JOHNSON CITY, N. Y.

44116

In 1913 the Johnson brothers (C. Fred, George F. and Harry L.) purchased 12 acres east of the Pioneer Factory and transformed it into a beautiful park area, since known as CFJ Park. The famous CFJ Pool was designed by Wesley Bintz, and was built in 1927. It was egg-shaped, could accomodate 2,000 bathers, and was one of the earliest above-ground pools in the country. It was demolished in 1982 by the Village, after an heroic effort by preservationists to save it.

1924

GEORGE F. JOHNSON SWIMMING POOL AND DANCING PAVILION, JOHNSON CITY, N. Y.   119019

The "George F. Pavilion" adjacent to the swimming pool in C.F.J. Park was built in 1926, of a modified Spanish design with a steel frame and a tapestry brick and limestone finish. Through the years in its service as a popular dance hall, practically all the 'big bands' of America have played there—Benny Goodman, Artie Shaw, The Dorsey Brothers, and many others. The admission price was always very nominal, $1 or so, and thus it was a very popular spot. Its floor can accomodate 1200 couples. Today it is known as "The Fountains Pavilion".

the area was known as Wagner Park. Around 1909 it was purchased by J. E. Gray and was renamed Riverside Park. A local music writer and publisher, Charles Cohen, wrote the famous 'Riverside Rag' and dedicated it to J. E. Gray; on the cover of the sheet music the park was depicted with the County Court House in the background. Late in 1910 the park was purchased by the Lestershire Bible Training School (now know as the Practical Bible Training School) and the area is now known as Bible School Park.

BIRD'S EYE VIEW LACKAWANNA STATION AND FACTORY DISTRICT, JOHNSON CITY, N. Y.

The forerunner of the Endicott-Johnson Shoe Company was the shoe manufacturing business started by H. N. Lester in 1850. The vast factories in this picture represent a small portion of the industrial empire that eventually flourished all over the Triple Cities and Owego. Note the Johnson City Lackawanna Railroad station at right center, and the spires of St. James Church at the extreme right.

Johnson City's first school building was built in 1891 at 47 Harrison Street; in 1900 it became the first home of the Practical Bible Training School. In 1911 Dr. Charles S. Wilson purchased it for the Lestershire Hospital and in later years it served as the Wilson Hospital School of Nursing.

JOHNSON CITY HOSPITAL, JOHNSON CITY, N. Y.

Architect Charles Edward Vosbury of Binghamton was called upon to design the Johnson City High School for two stages of development. The east half was constructed in 1914 with one tower, and it opened for classes in September of 1915. The second half was constructed about 13 years later. While superficially the building appears to be symmetrical, the west section is longer by the equivalent of one classroom, and the windows are 54 inches wide as compared with 48 inches on the older part. The original design called for a 600-seat auditorium; this was changed to 1000 seats in the final concept, and the gym was added. The entrance lobby was widened from the original plans, as were the steps, and this resulted in the flagpole and walkway not being centered as one might normally expect.

JOHNSON CITY HIGH SCHOOL, JOHNSON CITY, N. Y.   7A-H46

CENTRAL FIRE STATION AND ENDICOTT, JOHNSON & CO. FACTORY, JOHNSON CITY, N. Y.

The Johnson City Municipal Building still stands, although without its minaret-like tower. It was built in 1898-9 by James Sullivan, who constructed several other buildings in the village. A large community hall on the third floor was an important feature. The shoe factory on the left in the picture is the "Pioneer Annex", an addition to the first large "Pioneer Factory" of the E-J Corporation.

Johnson City's Fire Station, part of the municipal building as seen above, was dedicated November 1, 1899. In this dandy scene we see Chief Eldredge and C. Fred Johnson in the motorcar at the center, with the Police Ambulance (Black Maria) on their right. The officer on the motorcycle is Police Chief Hadden. The steam pumper is an American LaFrance of 1900 vintage, and the two other vehicles are Nott fire engines. Note the signs above the doors: Independent Hose Co., H. B. Endicott Steamer, C. F. Johnson Hose Co, and Rescue Hall. The steamer was lost to a World War II scrap drive, but the lanterns from it and the ornamental Eagle are known to have survived.

CENTRAL FIRE STATION, JOHNSON CITY, N. Y.

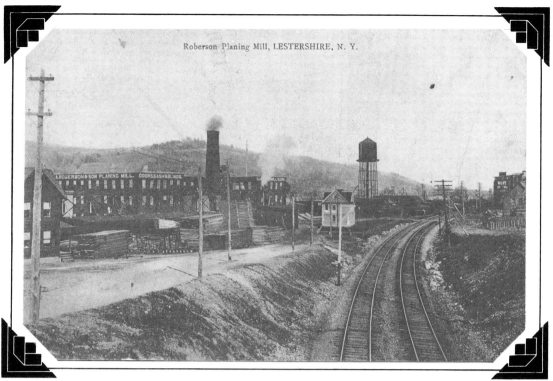

Roberson Planing Mill, LESTERSHIRE, N. Y.

In 1834 Norman Marsh came to Binghamton and started the manufacture of sash, blinds, and doors at his home on Chenango Street. About 1840 he built a small factory on Chenango Street, and soon was joined by a partner, George Flint. In a few years the firm of St. John and Gilbert succeeded to the proprietorship. This firm failed and in 1854 Alonzo Roberson, a former employee, purchased the plant. His successful business led to several business expansions. In 1893, he moved to the eastern edge of Lestershire where he erected several large buildings, and in the same year his son Alonzo Jr. became a partner with his father at a time when 200 men were employed. Alonzo Sr. died in 1899 and the firm continued under the son's management. He built a great mansion on Front Street in Binghamton, now the Roberson Center for the Arts and Sciences.

The Marshall Furniture Factory was in business from 1898 until 1911, and manufactured, among other things, lath, shingles, mouldings, redwood siding, doors, maple and oak flooring, and all the other items one might expect from a mill of this nature. This view is looking southeast from the corner of Willow and Corliss, now Ozalid property. A spur of the Erie railraod is seen in the front of the picture. The DL & W was in the front of the factory.

The Marshall Furniture Factory, LESTERSHIRE, N. Y.

THE FELTERS CO., LESTERSHIRE, N. Y.

The Felters Company at 80 Arch Street in Johnson City was established in 1890, as a result of uniting three felt companies—the Diedicke Company, the Bowden Felting Company, and the Footy Reynolds Company— and it was still making felt in the 1950's. Felts for all purposes were produced; for felt shoes, harness packs, gas-kets and washers and a myriad of other mechanical uses. Felt making consists of beating wet wool fibers to cause them to pack together; the more the wool is beat, the harder the product becomes. The building is now occupied by the Lescron Book Outlet, known in the book trade as a 'remainder house.'

Washingtonian Hall Near Binghamton, N.Y.

64256 Ⓜ

Amos Patterson, a man of influence in the Town of Union, built an impressive white clapboard house around 1800, and it stands to-day. In 1840 the Washington Temperance Society was founded in our nation's capital, and local auxiliaries were formed across the land to work against the use of strong drink. Adherents to its policies were known as 'Washingtonians'. In 1842, John Sayer, who had purchased the Patterson home in 1830 for use as a temperance inn (evidently a hotel where no liquor was sold) painted "Washingtonian Hall" in large letters on the building.

This picture of the International Time Recording Company, the forerunner of IBM, dates from around 1914, when the card was postmarked in Endicott. The firm had been formed by the combining in 1911 of the Computing-Tabulating Recording Company, the Tabulating Machine Company and the Computing Scale Company of America.

International Time Recording Co., Endicott, N. Y.

INTERNATIONAL BUSINESS MACHINE CORPORATION, ENDICOTT, N. Y.   7A-H4F

The IBM factory building on the northwest corner of North Street and McKinley Avenue in Endicott was dedicated on September 19, 1942, and is still very much in use. Why the company felt it necessary to have four United States flags flying—one to each of four buildings—is not clear, although possibly a patriotic fervor during World War II, when the picture was probably taken, had something to do with the display. Close inspection reveals that the flags are actually artist-imposed!

Chester B. Lord, Treasurer of the Endicott-Johnson Coporation, was the moving force behind the original 'Endicott Free Library' in 1915, which was started in a rented store. In 1918 E-J gave it financial support, and the home of Harlowe Bundy was purchased for a permanent home for the library. In 1950 the home of George F. Johnson (bottom picture) became the George F. Johnson Memorial Library, and it served the Village for 16 years until the present library at 1001 Park Street was opened.

ENDICOTT LIBRARY, ENDICOTT, N. Y.   76872

Geo. F. Johnson Residence, Endicott, N. Y.

In 1907 this was the home of George F. Johnson in Endicott, and it was probably designed by S. O. Lacey. This handsome and stately structure was razed in 1966, thus erasing forever one more famed landmark that hailed to the days of the founding of 'The Home of the Square Deal' in the Triple Cities. Once again we see many canvas awnings, a much-used protective measure against the summer's heat in pre-air-conditioning times.

40

ENDICOTT GENERAL HOSPITAL, ENDICOTT, N. Y.

Dr. Roger D. Mead operated Endicott's 50-bed fully-equipped hospital in the 'teens and '20s until Ideal Hospital was opened. It was located on the south side of Main Street, between Garfield and Grant Avenues. Dr. Mead's widow, Mae L. Mead, resided on the property until her death in December of 1981. The property was demolished in the mid-1980's.

George F. Johnson gave $150,000 towards construction of Ideal Hospital, which opened June 30, 1927. The total cost was $338,000, of which $38,000 came from individuals and societies. The nurses home opened in 1929, built by Mrs. George F. Johnson in memory of her sister, Mrs. Anna McGlore Harrington. The hospital was operated by the Village of Endicott until 1980. Currently it is the Ideal-Wilson Medical Center.

Ideal Hospital, Endicott, N. Y.

OB-H10F

Hotel Frederick, Endicott, N. Y.

Construction in Endicott started in 1904. Horses were still the predominant means of locomotion when this picture of Washington Avenue was made somewhere around 1910, when the trolley line was in business, but the surface of the road was still dirt. The Hotel Mix on the right is the building which currently houses the brokerage firm of Cheevers, Hand & Angeline.

George F. Johnson built the Frederick Hotel (named for C. Fred Johnson) and it opened for business on April 1, 1906. According to "History of Endicott" by James Fiori, "The original structure was of wood frame [construction] containing 12 rooms; in 1918 another 12 rooms were added. Annexes were put on in 1933, 1936, and 1948 to make a total of 94 rooms." The building was demolished in 1968.

Washington Ave., Endicott, N. Y.

Casino Entrance, Endicott.

Casino Park in Endicott, as depicted on this postcard which the post office cancelled on August 20, 1906, was in operation until 1915. The round building, as might be suspected, housed a carousel. In intervening years the place was labelled Ideal Park, and also En-Joie Park. It was sponsored by the Endicott-Johnson Corporation, and on this site is today's E. J. Office Building on the south side of Main Street, opposite Lincoln Avenue.

The Union-Endicott High School seen here was on Loder Avenue, and part of the structure remains, incorporated into the Jennie F. Snapp School.

Union-Endicott High School, Union, N. Y.

43

UPPER LEATHER TANNERY, ENDICOTT, JOHNSON & CO., ENDICOTT, N. Y.

In this building is tanned all grades of upper leather. The leather is tanned by a secret process, which adds to its strength and durability, insuring better wearing shoes. A daily capacity of 2,000 skins.

The Endicott-Johnson tannery on Clark Street in Endicott was alleged to be the largest in the World. Its construction in 1902 triggered the beginning and growth of Endicott. It was closed in 1966, and was razed in 1968.

SOUR VATS SOLE LEATHER TANNERY, ENDICOTT, JOHNSON & CO., ENDICOTT, N. Y.
More than a Million Dollars worth of hides continually in the operation of tanning.   Length of vat yard 600 ft.

RACE TRACK, IDEAL PARK, ENDICOTT, N. Y.

This race track, adjacent to En-Joie Park and the Endicott High School, was part of the Orange County Circuit. The horse barns seen in the far center right were built in 1920, and were demolished in 1962 for the construction of the Thomas J. Watson (McKinley Avenue) Bridge.

The popular Carmel Grove Methodist Campground in the Beatrice Lane area of the Town of Union, (not Binghamton, as printed on the postcard) was opened in 1872. Lots were sold for cottages or tents, and at one time there were as many as 400 of these on the grounds, as well as a three story hotel and a grocery store. Sunday attendances of 5000 were not unusual, and in 1896 an auditorium seating 1500 was erected. A chapel seating 300, a new water supply, acetylene lights, a new hotel and a telephone were added around the turn-of-the-century. On June 24, 1914, a heavy windstorm destroyed the auditorium, and effectively put the camp permanently out of business.

Row of Cottages, Carmel Grove, Binghamton, N. Y.

Ross Park was given to the City of Binghamton by Erastus Ross in 1875 and it was served by the Park Avenue street car line built in 1881. This line, which originally had horse-drawn cars, was electrified in 1887. The park, in addition to its natural beauties, had many amusement rides including a roller coaster, and a wide variety of entertainment acts were brought in for the amusement of the many patrons.

Prior to the days when automobiles were common, attractive amusement parks such as Ross Park provided a real social need for low-cost entertainment for the masses. Cheap trolley-car transportation to and from such parks made it easy for the average working man to take advantage of these facilities, and the lovely sylvan setting of this park made is especially attractive for residents of the community for picnics, outings, and general entertainment. Note what appears to be a bandstand on the right.

Ross Park, Binghamton, N. Y.

The fourth and present county court house was built in 1897-98, by Miles Leonard after designs by Isaac Perry. It may be that the patriotic bunting hung on the Court House and the other buildings in the area had to do with the Broome County Centennial.

Picture postcards were first authorized by the U.S. Post Office in 1892, coincident with the 1893 Columbian Exhibition in Chicago. For several more years the back side of the card was reserved exclusively for the address; any written message had to be on the face of the card. Congress amended the postal laws in 1907 so that messages were permitted on the back of the card instead of on the 'face', and a central dividing line indicated to postal patrons where they might write. This explains the writing adjacent to this scene of a large crowd at Courthouse square in Binghamton, on the occasion of the Broome County centennial in 1906. Note the monitor-topped trolley cars.

Chenango Street,
looking North,
Binghamton, N. Y.

Chenango Street, looking North from a spot just a stone's throw away from the scene in the other picture on this page, as it appeared on a postcard put in the mails in 1917. Note the interesting multi-globed street lights missing from the picture on page 52, which suggests it is a later view. An artist has carefully deleted all overhead wiring, which makes for a prettier picture, but does not explain how the trolley system was able to operate! The Symphony Theatre featured a small Link pipe organ to accompany the silent films of the day. At the far left are the White House Restaurant, the Binghamton Knitting Mills, Dean's Pharmacy (in the Moon Building), and the Kilmer Laboratories—today the Carlova properties. At the right is an old favorite watering hole of Binghamtonians for many years, the Carlton Hotel; the Arlington Hotel is just beyond it.

18. View from Court House, Binghamton, N. Y.

This picture of the corner of Court and Chenango Streets had to have been taken between 1904, when the Press Building was built (the tall building at the center), and 1908, when the top floor of the Phelps Building (at the right intersection) burned.

25.—FRATERNITY ROW, WASHINGTON STREET, BINGHAMTON, N. Y.

44530

Left to right on Binghamton's "Fraternity Row" are the New York State Armory, The Knights of Columbus, the Fraternal Order of Elks, and Kalurah Temple, owned by a Masonic Order. When the New York State Institute of Applied Arts and Sciences was burned out of the Armory in 1951, it occupied Kalurah Temple and two other nearby buildings for five years, after which it moved to a new campus on upper Front Street. By then its sponsorship had changed from New York State to Broome County, under provision of the new Community College Law, and its name has variously changed to "Broome County Technical Institute" and "Broome Technical Community College"; currently it is known as "Broome Community College." Kalurah Temple is now the Assembly of God Church.

Knights of Columbus Club House, Binghamton, N. Y.

The Frederick Lewis/Sidney T. Clark house at 123 Washington Street in Binghamton, appears in the scene above. It is thought to have been designed by Isaac Perry, around 1860. It became the home of the local Knights of Columbus in 1908, part of Washington Street's "Fraternity Row". and in later years various additions were made to the property. It was demolished in 1923, and today the site is a parking lot.

The radio tower on the left of the center picture was installed in 1913 by the Marconi Company, which pioneered the wireless telephone (today we call it radio) for railroads throughout the world. In the distant left is the Security Mutual Life Insurance Company building, and just to the right is the dome of the County Court House. Next is the spire of the First Presbyterian Church, followed by the Press Building. Note the construction activity at the left (east) end of the Arlington Hotel, and the fact that it has two more stories than the picture dated July 17, 1906. To its right is the George Q. Moon building, and then the Kilmer Laboratories, where "Swamp Root" was produced.

July 17, 1906.

CORNER CHENANGO AND LEWIS STREETS - BINGHAMTON, N.Y.

Will leave here Thursday on No. 2, & come to the Eddy. Mae.

View from Viaduct, Binghamton, N. Y.

The Viaduct, Binghai.

Notice that the Erie RR freight house has been added between 1906 and 1919. One of the most fascinating aspects of the study of postcards of any community is seeing what changes can be detected over various periods of time.

50

21:—Public Library, Binghamton, N. Y.

The Binghamton Public Library, built in 1904 as a gift of Andrew Carnegie, became the Broome County Public Library in 1985. The First Universalist Church at the right (in which the Christian Scientists were also permitted to meet) was built in 1893 and demolished in 1929 to make way for the Binghamton Savings Bank.

Monday Afternoon Club, Binghamton, N. Y.

Sherman Phelps had Isaac Perry design his house and his bank on Court Street at the same time, in 1870-71. As written by Margaret Axtell, "It was one of the city's most costly residences, in the best style of the later Victorian period. It was amply complemented with spacious lawns, flower beds, and fountains. The stable and carriage house shielded by trees bordered Pine Street. A Magnificent iron fence, product of the Titchener Iron Works, surrounded all with a gate on Fayette Street allowing carriages to enter the property and approach the rear porch. . . It was acquired by the Monday Afternoon Club in 1905 from John Stuart Wells.

Chenango Street as it appeared in the 'teens. The 12-story Press Building, built by Willis Sharpe Kilmer, housed his Binghamton Press which, as was typical of newspapers of the day, championed various causes in which he was interested. To its right is the Stone Opera House , then the Odd Fellows Hall (the postcard caption has these two mixed, and also has a 'P' inserted in the name of the City), the Central Fire Station, and Ned's Horse Shoe Cafe with the words 'Quick Lunch' emblazoned across the front end of the little structure. Close inspection with a glass reveals that the words printed vertically on either side of the door are 'LADIES' and 'GENTS', thus suggesting that even in that 'pre-women's lib' day the owner was taking no chances of being criticized for catering to one gender in favor over the other.

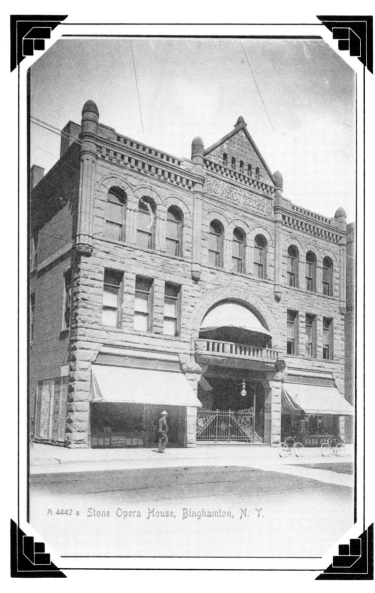

A 4442 a. Stone Opera House, Binghamton, N. Y.

Charles M. Stone built an opera house in 1892 on this site. It burned on October 9, 1903, and he rebuilt it as shown here. For many years it was the Riviera Theatre, which closed in the 1970's. In the mid 1980's it is being rebuilt as still another theatre, by the Sarkisian interests.

The Binghamton Central Fire Station on Chenango Street was built in 1896 at a cost of $10,000 for the site and $11,605 for the building. It was designed by A. W. Reynolds and built by Alexander B. Carman. In 1911 the Fire Department had three steam engines, one Nott and two by LaFrance—note that the dapple team on the right is harnessed to a steam pumper. Note also the sleigh, a feature not seen amongst today's fire fighting equipment. Prior to 1911 fires in the city were fought by volunteer fire companies; in that year the Fire Department was organized with a paid staff. Charles N. Hogg was the Chief Engineer, a term no longer used in the profession. Harry Eldredge, his assistant, later was hired by Endicott-Johnson to form a department in Johnson City and to ensure that their factories had top-notch protection from blazes such as the disasterous overall factory fire in Binghamton that cost so many lives in 1913.

3613 BINGHAMTON, N. Y.
Central Fire Station.

Crow Bar Hotel, Binghamton, N. Y.
Free Board to Guests. Visitors seldom admitted for less than Thirty Days.

The second Broome County jail, designed by Isaac Perry, was used from 1896 until 1939 when it was demolished to make way for the new County Office Building. It was toward the southeast corner of Court House Square, and here we see it from the east, with the tower of City Hall visible in the background. Note the reference to "free board to guests at the Crow Bar Hotel", etc. Part of the jail still exists in the form of a home near Castle Creek that was constructed from the stone transported from Court House Square.

There's not an automobile to be seen in this turn-of-the-century view of downtown Binghamton, and no one had to worry about parking ramps. Old Dobbin was still in evidence to haul the mails, and the monitor-topped trolley car is of early design in the annals of traction. While the streets may have been clear of carbon monoxide, the reader can be certain that tax monies a-plenty had to be spent to shovel up after the horses.

Washington Street N. Binghamton, N.Y.

1013. — Court Street Looking West, Binghamton, N.Y.

At left is the corner of Collier and Court, looking west. On the left is the McNamara Building of 1870, with a fine pedestal clock gracing the sidewalk. This building was replaced in 1916 with the Marine Midland Bank. Note the bicycles at the curb, and the many utility poles.

Arlington Hotel.
Binghamton, N. Y.

The Arlington Hotel was built in 1887 at Chenango and Lewis Streets. It underwent many additions and changes between then and 1967 when it was demolished in the name of "urban renewal"; in 1985 the lot was still empty. T. I. Lacey was probably the architect of the original building, and at least some of the additions. Originally there was a tower on this near corner. One of the additions is evident at the left of the building.

Hotel Bennett, Binghamton, N. Y.

Binghamton's first mayor, Abel Bennett, built this hotel on Washington Street in 1881. It housed a barber shop and public baths—with special hours for ladies. At one period it was known as the Bingham Hotel; it was demolished in 1965 to make way for "Urban Renewal"; the lot was vacant until 1984 when the Metrocenter opened.

COURT STREET LOOKING SOUTH BY NIGHT,
BINGHAMTON, N. Y.

Closed automobile bodies did not become popular until the early 1920's, so these cloth-topped touring cars suggest that the scene is from the 'teens in downtown Binghamton. The vast array of lights in the buildings indicate that there was plenty of business to be done after daytime hours. Note the flagpole on the tower of the Boston store (Fowler's) building; for years a pennant flying on it indicated that there was a Triplet baseball game in town that day. Once again, an artist has shown his disdain for the niceties of traction technology by carefully air-brushing out the overhead wires needed to power the trolley cars, seen in the distance, right by the Chenango River. And of course, the scene looks west, not south, as the caption writer would have us believe.

Binghamton, N. Y.
Boston Store.

The "Boston Store"/Fowlers was built in 1899 by James O'Neill, with Sanford O. and Halbert A. Lacey as architects. In 1971 the tower was removed and a modern brick siding added. The Fowler Store closed in 1981; the building was re-opened in 1984, after extensive renovation and modernization, as Boscov's Department Store.

Prior to 1883 Battery C of the 104th Field Artillery was housed in convenient barns, but during that year it was moved into this new Armory at #202 to #212 State Street. At this time the canal which was to become State Street had not been filled, and the artillerymen were forced to use their ingenuity to provide a system of skids to get their ordnance into the canal and out and into the building. During the years since 1905 the building has served a variety of purposes. It has been a hotel (Augustus Wales, prop.) and a theatre, as noted on the card, as well as at least one automobile agency, and a parking garage. Currently the Roger White Advertising and Public Relations agency occupies space in the building, as does the Wilcox Floor Covering business.

The New York State Armory on Washington Street in Binghamton was the second one in the city, and was built in 1905. In 1946 it became the first home of the New York State Institute of Applied Arts and Sciences, with Cecil C. Tyrrell as its founding director; eventually this school became Broome Community College. The structure was totally destroyed by fire on Labor Day weekend in 1951, and a Binghamton fire fighter lost his life in the blaze.

The Paige house, "Riverside", where Lewis and Washington Streets join. It was designed by Isaac Perry, and was built by D. J. Sullivan in 1874. It became the YWCA in 1897, and rooms were added on the west side. In 1920 it became the Georgian Hotel.

The Binghamton YMCA was razed in the 1970's as part of a downtown 'renewal' project. The structure next to it in this picture was the Christ Episcopal Church Rectory from about 1885, and later the Guild House to the late 1930's or early '40s, when it was razed. Built at 101 Washington Street, it was the home of Samuel J. Olmstead from 1867.

The Wilkinson Block was built in 1892, with Audley W. Reynolds as architect. It burned in 1941, but the lower level was saved and now houses the Walter Shoe Company.

5165   LADY JANE GREY SCHOOL. BINGHAMTON. N.Y.   PUBL. BY LESTER ART NOVELTY CO.

The Lady Jane Grey School was what is known as a 'Finishing School', and it operated for the benefit of young ladies from 'upper crust' families from a wide area—not just Broome County, from 1861 to 1923. This structure was built in 1810 at Court and Liberty Streets by Joshua Whitney. For a time it served as the Brandywine Hotel. It was demolished in 1926 for the gas works. Perhaps its greatest claim to fame is that it was attended by Alice Jane Chandler Webster, (1876-1916) who wrote novels and plays under the name Jean Webster, and who used the setting of the school for her most famous book Daddy Long Legs (1912) which was made into three films starring Mary Pickford (1919), Janet Gaynor (1931) and Fred Astaire and Leslie Caron (1955). Ms. Webster went on to Vassar College after her stint at Lady Grey's establishment.

New High School. Binghamton, N. Y.

The Binghamton High School was built in 1913-14 for $600,000 to designs by Charles Edward Vosbury, as were so many other structures in the city, and it opened in 1915. Extensive renovations and additions were made in the 1980's.

6:—MASONIC TEMPLE. BINGHAMTON, N. Y.

The Masonic Temple at Main and Murray Streets was built in 1922, at a cost of $350,000 and it contained three Binghamton-made Beman pipe organs used for various Masonic functions. The architects were Walter H. Whitlock and Charles H. Conrad. This was also the home of the Tri-Cities Opera for several years.

38:—Binghamton Club, Binghamton, N. Y.

Binghamton, N.Y. Binghamton Club.

The Binghamton Club was established on Nov. 20, 1880, by 39 founding members. The club originally met in rooms rented from the City National Bank at the corner of Court and Washington Streets. Its location varied from time to time, meeting in 1886 in the Perry Block at the corner of Court and Chenango Streets, in 1892 in the Strong Block at the corner of State and Henry Streets, to its location for 23 years in the multi-dormered building seen above at the corner of Henry and Chenango Streets. The Board of Governors began plans for the clubhouse at its present location at 83 Front Street in February 1923. It was opened in September of 1924, and was described by The Morning Sun of August 5, as "a Georgian colonial with oriental rugs, colonial furniture, . . card rooms, billiard rooms, and lounges." In the 1960's a wing was added to the front, replacing the portico seen above, the bequest of insurance man Conrad Klee.

The Griffith mansion, 'River Mound", was a fine Italian Villa on Binghamton's South Side. In 1871 it became the Susquehanna Valley Home, for underprivileged youth. It was razed in 1956 to make room for modern home "cottages" for its clientele, after having served for 85 years.

St. Paul's Elementary School was built in 1923, on Doubleday Street, behind St. Paul's Roman Catholic Church. It ceased to operate as a Catholic Parochial school in 1976, and was demolished in 1985.

The Delaware, Lackawanna, and Western Railroad Station was built in 1901, together with 7 other freight and passenger stations elsewhere on the line that year. It is very similar in appearance to the station at Newark, New Jersey. It has been said that mile for mile, the Lackawanna was the most highly developed railroad in America! This picture was taken shortly after the station was opened, judging by the styles of the few automobiles present. The architect was Samuel Huckel who maintained offices on Park Avenue in New York City. In 1985 the structure was purchased by architects Peter Trozze and James Bryden from Conrail, with the intent to develop offices and stores after rehabilitating the structure. The purchase price was $130,000.

D. L & W. R. R. Station, Binghamton, N. Y.

This picture was taken from the Chenango Street viaduct, which was built in 1901. The Erie tracks are on the right; they were built in 1848 on open farm lands north of the main part of the city. The Delaware and Hudson tracks (originally the Albany and Susquehanna) are on the left. Note the gas holder in the background, and also the caboose at the left, which appears to be a four-wheel bobber from the mid-19th century. The structure at the center is an interlocking tower to prevent cars from either the D & H or the Erie freight yards from entering onto the Erie main line. The D & H freight house on the left was built in 1902 by Sullivan and Bagby Contractors. The Erie freight house is on the right.

Erie Railroad Yards, Binghamton, N. Y.

Binghamton, N.Y., Post Office.

In 1942 the Post Office (or Federal Building) which was built in 1891 on the corner of Wall and Henry Streets, was demolished. It suffered damage in the terrible clothing factory fire in 1913 because of the close proximity of the blaze, and further damage in the floods of the mid 'thirties. Between the river and the row of buildings is Wall Street. At left is the Post Office, and to its right stood the Clock and Son Cigar Factory, later the Freeman Overall Factory which burned in 1913 with a heavy loss of life; Barlow, Rogers & Simpson Cigar Factory; Wright, O'Connor & Co, Cigar Factory, and commercial buildings facing Court Street over one of which was the Y.M.C.A. which owned the building from 1883 to 1906. These latter two were replaced by The Fair Store. To the left of the Post Office is the area being developed by the Sarkisian interests as a Sheraton Hotel and Convention Center.

East Bank of Chenango River. Binghamton, N. Y.

3616 BINGHAMTON, N. Y. High School.

The Gothic-Italianate-styled Binghamton High School was built in 1870 at a cost of $100,000. It was torn down in 1913 to make room for the present school. Like many other structures in the region, it was designed by Isaac Perry.

Serie 1222: Ely's Tower, Binghamton, N. Y.

Ely Park and its famous tower was created by S. Mills Ely. He had donated lumber for construction of a temple for a traveling evangelist; when this was no longer needed he used the lumber to construct this tower on his mountain park northwest of the city of Binghamton. The park was donated to the city in 1907; subsequently the tower was destroyed in a windstorm.

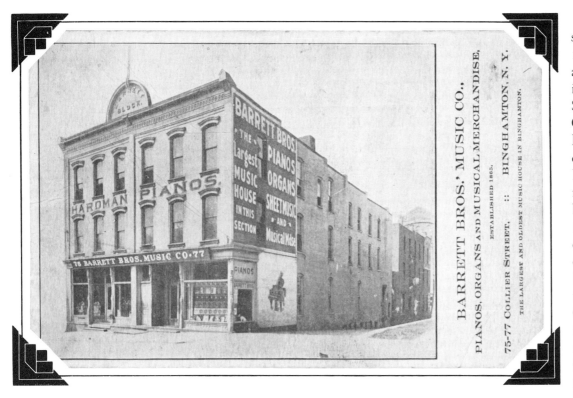

BARRETT BROS.' MUSIC CO.,
PIANOS, ORGANS AND MUSICAL MERCHANDISE,
ESTABLISHED 1865.
75-77 COLLIER STREET, :: BINGHAMTON, N. Y.
THE LARGEST AND OLDEST MUSIC HOUSE IN BINGHAMTON.

Barrett Brothers Music Store was founded in 1865. In this card as it appeared around 1910, it was at 75-77 Collier Street, next to the old City Hall—now the Hotel DeVille. Among other goods, Barrett Brothers sold Regina music boxes, presumably in the period from 1895 to 1919. This company eventually became the Weeks and Dickinson Music Store, which operated on Chenango Street until it closed in 1977. In the 1876 Atlas of Broome County, a scene inside this building is noted as S. W. Barrett's "Temple of Music and Jewelry."

The McLean Building, long known as "The Perry Block", as it was designed, built, and owned by architect Isaac Perry, who lived in an apartment on the top floor. This building is of cast iron construction; not too many of this type are left, and it was the only one in Broome County. Perry designed many buildings in the city, including the Court House, the Phelps Bank Building (at the right of this picture), Sisson's Department Store, The Public Library, The Fair Store, the Hotel Bennett, and the Centenary and Congregational Churches. The building is now listed on the National Historic Register, largely because it is an outstanding example of a cast-iron building.

HILLS, McLEAN & HASKINS STORE, BINGHAMTON, N. Y.

66

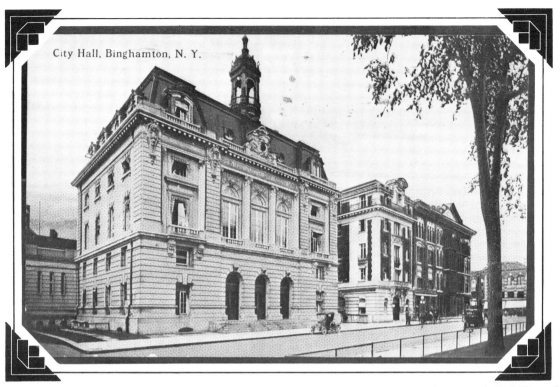

City Hall, Binghamton, N. Y.

Now the Hotel DeVille, the City Hall on Collier Street was built in 1897-8. Its Architect was Raymond Francis Almirall of Ingle & Almirall, a New York City firm. He graduated from Cornell, then studied in Paris, thus the French Renaissance Beaux Arts style of his efforts. The building is on the National Register of Historic Places, and was saved only by heroic efforts on the part of local preservationists.

BINGHAMTON
SAVINGS BANK BUILDING
BINGHAMTON, N. Y.

The Savings Bank building was constructed in 1897-8 next to and while the City Hall was being built. The Court House was being built at the same time, a busy time for central Binghamton.

The Salvation Army Citadel at 131 Washington Street was built around 1904. It was added to at various times, and in 1959 the exterior was modernized. It continues to serve the needy.

Binghamton Lodge #852, Fraternal Order of Elks, was initiated on May 28, 1903, with 28 members. Its meetings were held at 153 Washington Street, Binghamton, in the old Shrine Hall. Within a year, the Lodge purchased this 5-story brick building at 137 Washington Street with only $200 in the treasury and 88 members; the first meeting there was on May 30, 1904. In 1907, a large addition was made on the rear of the building, and the top four floors were by then used for Lodge activities. The first floor of the building for years served as a restaurant; many local diners have fond memories of "the Hub" delicatessen. In 1919 ground was purchased at 249 Washington Street for a new Lodge building, and construction was started there in 1922, with occupancy beginning on May 20 of 1924. In 1928 the Lodge had 2336 members. Note that the buildings in these two scenes adjoin. Harvey Singer restored both of the buildings in the picture at the right in the early 1980's.

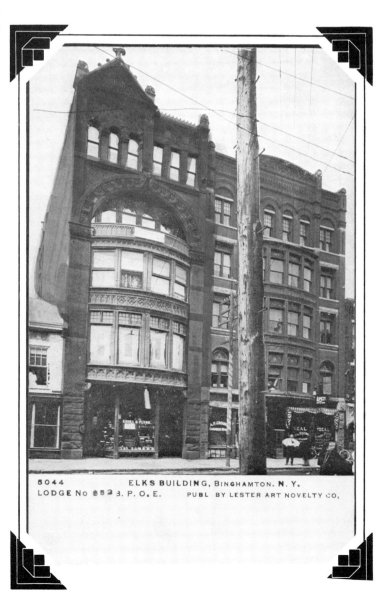

13. Chenango and Court Streets, Binghamton, N. Y.

The Phelps office building on the corner of Court and Chenango Streets in Binghamton was designed by the famed architect Isaac Perry. The top floor burned in 1908. In 1929 the First National Bank took over the building. There has been a bank on this corner for 150 years.

A parade at Court and Chenango Streets. This had to have taken place after 1908, because the top floor of the Phelps Building had already burned. Judging by the style of dress of the ladies at the curb, the photo is probably very close to that date.

Court House Square, Binghamton, N. Y.

+:—Sisson Bros. and Weldon Store, Binghamton, N. Y.

The front building was built in 1864 and was known as the "Granite Block". The 8-story addition was built in 1916-17, and the old granite building was faced to match. Sisson Brothers and Weldon operated a store here starting in 1859. The building was taken over by the Nezelek interests in 1964, and currently it is the home of the Key Bank.

O'Neil Building, Binghamton, N. Y.

The O'Neil building at State and Court Streets was built around 1875 as the Ross Block and it housed the Merchant's National Bank, with Erastus Ross as its President—the same Ross who donated Ross Park. Currently it houses the Chemical Bank of New York on its ground floor. This scene is around 1914. The Drazen store for women's wear operated in this building for many years.

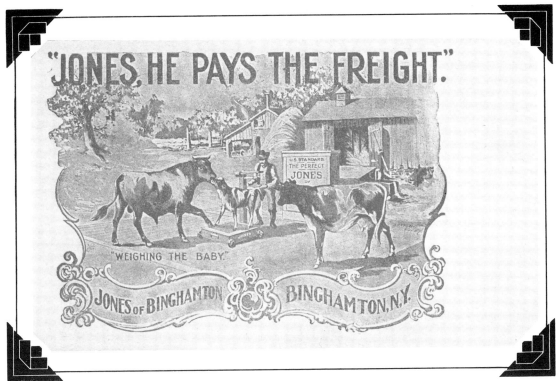

"JONES, HE PAYS THE FREIGHT."

"WEIGHING THE BABY."

JONES of BINGHAMTON   BINGHAMTON, N.Y.

The Jones Scale Works was organized in 1865 by General Edward F. Jones, and by 1885 it employed 100 men and its scales were well known throughout the country. For many years it was one of Binghamton's leading industries, employing as many as 300. The company initiated the policy of paying the freight charges on its products, and the motto "Jones, He Pays the Freight" was born, and became widely known. A prominent citizen, Jones was the first President of the Binghamton City Hospital which was organized in 1887, a member of the first Binghamton Water Commission (organized 1887), and a member of the first Park Commission, which was organized after Erastus Ross had donated 100 acres of land to the city for a park—known since as Ross Park.

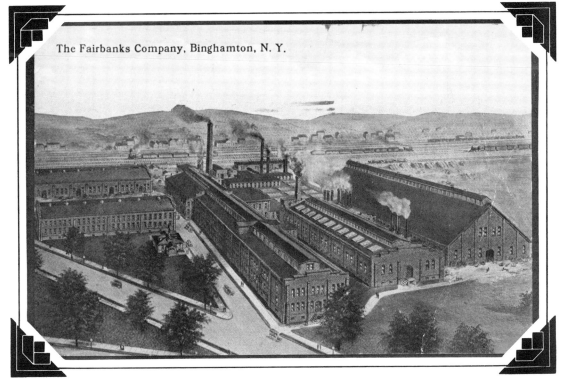

The Fairbanks Company, Binghamton, N. Y.

Fairbanks Company history can be traced back to 1837. The plant on Glenwood Avenue in Binghamton was originally the Demarest Stove Company, but in 1909 it became the Georgian Manufacturing Company— later changed to the Fairbanks Company. Up to the 1920's Fairbanks was best known by the scales which it had long made and for which a World-Wide trade had been established. In recent years the primary product has been valves, but in an earlier day hand trucks, transmission appliances, and general mechanical supplies ranging from pullies to marine engines have been produced. The company was sold to a competing firm in 1984 and the plant was closed.

71

The Security Mutual Building in the distance was built in 1903, and the company invested almost all of its assets in the structure—something no insurance company would be permitted to do today. Its water-powered hydraulic elevators for many years were of interest to students of technical devices. Elevators of this construction require a piston going into the ground a distance equal to the height of the building.

A Hundred Years Ago - - - and Today

Two views of Court Street in Binghamton, N. Y., taken from the Chenango River Bridge, showing the change a century has wrought.
Trolleys shown now replaced by Speed Buses; loading platforms removed and streets resurfaced.

BINGHAMTON CENTENNIAL CELEBRATION

This card heralds the 1934 Centennial commemoration of the incorporation of the Village of Binghamton. At left is an 1810 view of Court Street looking east to Court House Hill. The drawing was executed in 1834 by George Park, as he remembered the scene.

72

BINGHAMTON, N. Y., RIVERSIDE DRIVE.

Riverside Drive, just west of the Chenango River. At right is the mansion built by Jonas M. Kilmer at the turn-of-the-century. Quoting from a history assembled by the Junior League: "This majestic residence overlooking the Susquehanna River, designed by Charles Edward Vosbury, took three years to build. A cross between Italian Renaissance and Queen Anne, the quarry cut stone hid a palace of richness. . . The Kilmer estate stretched over 100 acres along the Susquehanna River. After the death of Jonas in 1912 and his wife Julia one year later, the house remained vacant but was meticulously maintained by his son and daughter-in-law." Since 1950 it has been the property of Temple Concord, the Jewish Liberal Reformed Synagogue.

Chenango Street above Bevier Street, Binghamton, N. Y.

Chenango Street, looking north. Note the brick pavement and the double track of the trolley line. Originally the Port Dickinson Railway, it later became the Binghamton Railway.

Transportation has always been a key factor in the development of cities, and Binghamton is no exception. At the confluence of two rivers, the Chenango and the Susquehanna, it was a natural spot for early settlement. It eventually became a railroad hub, with the Lackawanna, the Albany and Suquehanna (later the Delaware and Hudson), the Erie, and the Lehigh Valley railroads all serving the economic base of the community. In the 1960s and 70s Interstate Highways 81 and 88 and the 'Southern Tier Expressway'—New York Route 17, converged in Binghamton, to provide further reason for continued development. But through it all, the rivers have continued to provide unmatched beauty, as suggested in this bucolic scene of a less hectic time.

Binghamton, N.Y., Susquehanna River & Boat House.

From 1864 to 1901 this was the home of Horace Lester (of the Lester Shoe Company, the forerunner of the Endicott-Johnson Corporation), at 60 Main Street. From 1903 to 1919 it was the Cyrus Strong house after his home at Court and Chenango was razed. After 1920 it housed the Daughters of Isabella, and later the Catholic Daughters of America until 1929 when it was demolished by the Standard Oil Company.

22:—CATHOLIC DAUGHTERS OF AMERICAN (D. OF ISABELLA), BINGHAMTON, N. Y.

12237

City Hospital, Binghamton, N.Y.

This is the second City Hospital building, and it served in that capacity from 1895 until 1913. Later it became the administrative office building for the hospital.

31:—View in South Side Park, Binghamton, N.Y.

Binghamton's South Side Park, showing the Washington Street "bowstring truss" in the background, as it appeared in the mid-'twenties, if one is to judge by the presence of the closed-body automobile. The styling of the ladies' garb would suggest an earlier date, and this is probably true as the car is an obvious out-of-perspective implant by whoever published the postcard. Cards of that era were frequently faked in this manner, and postcard collectors take great delight in spotting them!

This view of the highway bridge crossing the river from Conklin to Kirkwood is on the south side, looking west, at a spot just southeast of Binghamton. Today this crossing is accomplished by a modern structure which passes over the railroad, and which connects directly to Interstate Route 81.

THE BRIDGE
KIRKWOOD—CONKLIN
NY

RBER'S COFFEE DEN, 5 MILES NORTH OF BINGHAMTON, ON SYRACUSE HIGHWAY, RTE. 11   G-4

The late 1920's and the 1930's were a time when Americans were learning to 'take to the road'. Automobiles were becoming reliable and comfortable, roads were being paved, and fuel was cheap—so we were all for travelling hither and yon. All this meant that there was a living to be made by operating roadside establishments for feeding hungry motorists and fueling empty gas tanks, with the result that thousands and thousands of places just like Barber's Coffee Den opened all over America. Note the prices on the sign— dinners 50 cents, sandwiches 20 cents, etc.

The State Hospital campus, looking west. This site was once considered by Ezra Cornell for a university he was planning to found, said school eventually being located in Ithaca.

Binghamton, N.Y.,
Birdseye View showing State Hospital.

Built in 1858, this was the first hospital in the United States (and possibly the World) to look upon alcoholism as a sickness. It was known as the "Inebriate Asylum". It operated as such until 1879 when it was converted to a hospital for the mentally disturbed. It brought fame to its designer, Isaac G. Perry, and he was chosen to be the architect of the State Capitol in Albnay for the last 11 years of its construction. Note the towers, which have long since been removed, from the original "castellated gothic" design.

Binghamton, N.Y., State Hospital.   Cobb Photo.

The east end of Binghamton as seen from State Hospital hill. Note the D.L. & W. Railroad bridge crossing the Susquehanna River, and the large gas holder at the far center. This enormous structure at the corner of Court and Brandywine could be seen from all directions, and it was a convenient landmark for local aviators for the years from 1927 to 1969, when it was demolished. The development of underground storage techniques utilizing previously-depleted gas fields rendered the large cylinder obsolete and a burden on the rate base and tax structure of the Columbia Gas Corporation.

WASHINGTON STREET BRIDGE BY NIGHT, BINGHAMTON, N.Y.

This bridge, as seen in a postcard view postmarked in 1917, is the longest multiple span parabolic truss in New York State. It is the patented design of William O. Douglas of Binghamton, and was built by the Berlin Bridge Company of East Berlin, Connecticut, in 1888. This construction is sometimes referred to as a "bowstring truss."

33.- Erie Depot and R. R. Y. M. C. A., Susquehanna, Pa.

The gothic-styled brick Erie depot in Susquehanna, Pennsylvania, as it appeared in 1910, is the nation's last outstanding example of a station hotel. The hotel, the Starrucca House, closed in 1903 and its great vaulted dining room was demolished. The City of Susquehanna acquired the 110-year-old building in 1975, and has since sold it to Mike Matis, a developer who has re-opened it as the Starrucca House, with a bar and dining facilities.

Steamer ERMINIE (Built - 1894-95 - Burned 1900.)
Plied the Susquehanna between Lanesboro, Pa. and The Islands.

2580/160   Art-tone Series by C. D. Burton, Lanesboro, Pa.   German

The Starrucca Viaduct, just south of Binghamton at Lanesboro, Pennsylvania is the largest stone railway bridge in that state. 1040 feet long, 90 to 100 feet high, 25 feet wide at the top and with seventeen arches, it was designed by A. Burton Cohen for the Erie Railway. James Kirkwood, for whom the town of Kirkwood is named, (and also Kirkwood, Missouri) was the resident engineer. When built, in 1848, it was the longest bridge on what was then the World's longest railway; it cost about $335,000. On October 14, 1973, the viaduct was named a National Historic Civil Engineering Landmark.

Bridge showing Court House in Distance from South Hill.
Owego, N. Y.

This view of the Owego Bridge looks north, to the Tioga County Court House. The bridge was built in 1891, and has since been replaced by a more modern one. When it was built it replaced a four span open wooden bridge which may have been destroyed in a flood, as were so many of its type in those days. The two court house towers visible in this picture are 115 feet high. In 1931 they were shortened to 92 feet, and the mansard design changed to a simple pitched construction. There are now four similar towers on the building. The cornerstone of the court house was laid in 1871, and the building was completed in 1873.

Owego's Central School at 231 Main Street was built in 1910 of pink brick, and was referred to by local wags as the "Pink Prison." While it was called a 'Central School', it always served as an elementary school. It ceased to be used for school purposes in 1975, and now it is called the Human Services Building and houses some State and Federal offices.

8581. Central School, Owego, N. Y.

80

Home for Aged Women, Owego, N. Y.

This structure at 369 Front Street is now a private home with apartments. In 1912 it was willed by Miss Anna Dean to the churches of Owego to be used as a home for aged women. At the inception of this usage, it was managed by 2 ladies from each of five churches—Baptist, Episcopal, Methodist, Congregational, and Presbyterian—ten in all!

8585. Coburn Free Library, Owego, N. Y.

The Coburn Free Library, originally named the Coburn-Hewitt Library when it was built in 1911, is still very much in use at its 275 Main Street location.

The Ah-wa-ga Hotel, Owego, N. Y.

The Ah-Wa-Ga Hotel, at the corner of Front and Lake Streets, was build in 1852, and was razed in 1957 to make room for today's Chase Lincoln Bank. In its earlier years it was the social center of the village. Older residents recall that when John D. Rockefeller visited the area and county of his birth, he stayed in the hotel. As youngsters they soon learned of the dimes that he always handed out to kids, and they converged at the hotel to get theirs.

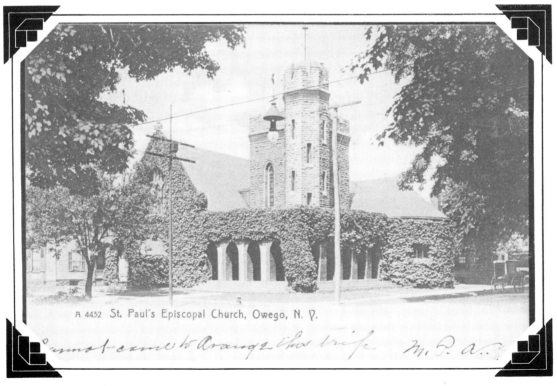

A 4432 St. Paul's Episcopal Church, Owego, N. Y.

St. Paul's Episcopal Church was built in 1893 on the northwest corner of Liberty and Main Streets, in what was then an orchard of the Pumpelly farm, at a cost of $12,800. It is constructed of bluestone with inner walls of cream colored brick. On the west side of the structure is the parish house which was given by Mrs. Louise Van Nostrand, in memory of her son, John James Van Nostrand of Brooklyn, New York, who died of the flu in 1906. Notice the interesting old street lighting fixture.